THROUGH
TROUBLED
WATERS

D1535416

Fear not for I have redeemed thee.
I have called thee by thy name, thou art mine.
When thou passest through the waters, I will be with thee;
and through the rivers, they shall not overflow thee. . . .
ISAIAH 43:1-2

THROUGH TROUBLED WATERS

William H. Armstrong

Abingdon Press

THROUGH TROUBLED WATERS

A Festival Book

Copyright © 1957, 1973, by William H. Armstrong

ISBN 0-687-41895-X

(previously published
by Harper & Row
under ISBN 0-06-060303-8)

Printed in the United States of America

To MARTHA who can never die

Author's Note

At this printing of *Through Troubled Waters*, the years have become decades since Martha Armstrong ceased walking the earth and left her legacy of love for that earth and all God's creatures. She left too her legacy of faith which has sustained us in our walking to look beyond the hills, however steep they rise before us, to the horizon beyond, to search for Abraham's city "which hath foundations, whose builder and maker is God."

The sun has risen over Segar Mountain more than eleven thousand times and many years. Days stirred up, shaken loose from night, and given brightness and new hope. And days growing and becoming permanent in weeks and months and memory. Gray Novembers have come bringing the death of the flowers. But an equal number of Aprils have returned after the winter, and the flowers with them. New generations of sheep have led their lambs to search the life-giving green that springs first from the damp spots in the pasture.

In these years there have been school years and working years. For little children they move at a witheringly slow pace; but finally toward maturity and a consciousness that Abraham's journey is everymen's journey. One with his mother's legacy of love and faith concerns himself with the heart discolorations of men and the human condition, and becomes a teacher of criminology and sociology. The other two, with that same legacy, become artists, painting the glorious creation, because they are convinced that there is never enough awareness of the beauty we are given to enjoy and revere.

Kent, Connecticut
1983

Contents

I

Cloud Patterns

If Indian Summer laps over into November, the latter days of November are often gray days. The cooling earth blends with the gray of the leafless trees, and only an occasional chrysanthemum hints that Persephone is delaying her steps into the dark cavern. The twenty-first of November was a gray autumn day. One best remembers such a day if he watches it after the sightless dark of a sleepless night.

The sky formed gray and hard. Some days have a firmness that lack even a fold of a bending, moving cloud. There seems a rigid strength in the inverted bowl of steel. It is a day that will remain as it begins.

There is time to watch a day build up if you have to stay in bed. The doctor was keeping me in bed for ten days. Mumps is no lark at forty.

I heard the sheep bells as the sheep, going down to the lower pasture, passed on the hillside. They would nibble at the gray sod for an hour and then pass again as they moved toward their favorite resting place at the south side of the shed. Five of the sheep were belled. Five Swiss bells, each with an individual tone, are pleasant if a man has time to listen. One bell was for Christopher, one for David, one for Mary, one for Mommy, and one for Daddy. On this particular morning the bells seemed to make a music that echoed the beginning of our glorious adventure which had turned a hill into a home. There were none of the somber notes which might foretell that the gray of the day would soon overcloud our lives.

Just a week ago the last of many big jobs had been finished. A strong woven-wire fence now surrounded all the land. The posthole digger and the wire stretcher were still at the northeast corner of the boundary. Now the sheep were secure against prowling dogs.

A sense of security gives a man a warm feeling inside. He hides from himself the fact that the warmth is from a selfish shell of his own making that has wrapped itself around him. I felt a warmth which I called security. I really wouldn't miss ten days from my teaching. This was Saturday, so Sunday wouldn't count for classes missed. Thanksgiving would be next week and the boys would go home Wednesday for four days. I would miss only five days of teaching. September and October are hellish months, getting schoolboys adjusted and organized, so I needed this rest. I could lie here and dream.

We had first looked at this rocky Connecticut hillside when the old apple trees were in bloom. Could we buy it? Standing four hundred feet up on this bony ridge, one looked down the Housatonic Valley for five miles to a point where Long Mountain and Bull's Bridge Mountain closed the vista below the sky. But the sky went on and on. The sound of the rapids, four hundred feet below, came up to us. How many nights their gentle roar would lull us to sleep. We would in time become so accustomed to them that no sound came up.

Could trees be cut and sawed and lumber piled to dry? Could stone be hauled in for chimneys and terraces? Now I smile, for other gray November days had seen me rush from school, dash past the apartment to leave a brief case, grab a crosscut saw, and hurry to the woods. On Thanksgiving Day six years ago a large hemlock had fallen the wrong way and lodged against a hickory. Would I have nerve enough now to cut the hickory and run as both trees started to fall? I wouldn't be so foolish again—or would I? Getting logs off rocky mountainsides is the hardest job a man can tackle. Every joint in your body is jolted to get the proper bite for the cant hook, and then to move the log requires muscles that were never even put in your body. But twenty-two thousand board feet of beautiful clean lumber is reward enough, and you have handled it so much that you can almost tell each board where it grew.

Sometimes people plant seeds of discouragement. "How will you ever get up that hill?" The first load of cement blocks came for the foundation and they avalanched slowly off the back of the truck. Long after dark I finished carrying up the three hundred and sixty-third block. It could have been worse; there were five hundred on the truck. After that, blocks and materials of all kinds were securely chained before the climb began.

It's still an hour before anyone will start to move around upstairs.

The children had seen their rooms studded in. They had placed blocks across the doorways and refused one another admittance. David had fallen through the hole left in the first floor for the chimney. I had picked him up in the basement. Blood spurted out of the top of his head. If you live in a small village, it is hard to find a doctor at eight-thirty, Saturday night, in the middle of summer. But there was no concussion, and all that remains of the one accident of the whole project is a wide place near the end of David's neatly trained part.

A man feels satisfied with the security he has hewn out of a hill. How did I ever get the first pair of rafters in place? They were sixteen feet long. They were strong and heavy and rest gently at the top against a fifty-foot ridgepole. The remembering of those rafters makes me tired even now, but it's all finished. The paneling has mellowed these three years, and already the house looks lived in. Someday I'll put the baseboard in the downstairs closets and line the window seat in our room with cedar. Then everything will be finished.

People have long since stopped asking, "How will they ever get up that hill?" The drive curves gently to take out the harshness of the incline. Half-inch stone embedded in asphalt gives the necessary traction in winter. We've developed a rock garden at the foot of the drive. Soon now we will build a board fence along each side of the driveway and the boys will have something to whitewash. I'll panel the little summerhouse with some elm boards I have drying in the shop, and perhaps build in two bunks for the boys. Then I'll go to all the places, and do all the things I've promised Martha all these busy years.

The gray morning holds. The day is typically late November. The sheep have been in the lower pasture an hour; the bells tell me they are coming around the hill. It's time Martha and the children were up and about.

My door is opened very gently. Martha looks in.

"I have been awake most of the night," I announce. "My temperature is high, I think, but the doctor said to expect that."

"I'll keep the children quiet so you can rest," Martha whispers. "Kip and David are invited out so it will be a reasonably quiet day. I want to get the rest of the shopping done for Thanksgiving, and go by the gift shop with Mary and let her pick out invitations for her birthday party. I'll bring your breakfast after the children are fed."

"I've just been lying here reviewing some of the hard work of the past," I muse. "I find myself snugly satisfied with the prospect of staying in bed for ten days."

"This is only the second day," Martha cautions. "You'll be unbearable before the ten have passed."

The children look in, but are quickly hurried away. Martha goes about her morning's work. She brings her coffee in and sits with me to drink it. She tells me that the weather report says the cloudy weather will continue. She talks of our going to Maryland for Thanksgiving with her father. I tell her I am sorry to have ruined the plan. She says it is all right. She'll write him tonight.

Routine filled up the morning; the shopping was done. The birthday invitations were brought home and put in the top drawer of the sewing table. They are still there. The boys went to play and lunch with their friends, Mike and Jeff Greiner. My temperature rose slightly during the morning. Hourly the sheep went past to graze. I listened to the bells.

The afternoon was the other half of a gray November day. The Porzelts, neighbors from the mountain, came by for a visit with Martha. They left a biography of George Sand for us to read. Cliff and Edith Loomis came at dusk. He always takes care of the chickens and sheep when I am sick. He is one of my teaching associates, and a neighbor who knows what "neighbor" means.

Finally the gray darkened and the day, so like many another in late November, ended. There was, however, a difference. This was our last day together.

II

Flood

The waters rise almost imperceptibly and without notice. Around a tree or embankment there is a whirling, gentle and silent. Sometimes the silence is broken with a muffled laughterlike sound as the water dances with the thing it will destroy. Then almost without sound, except a faint gurgling swallow, the tree or the embankment slips into the flood and is no more.

Martha kept a diary. She wrote five lines a day with nothing more important than: "Smoky Smith here to play; Libby came for him and visited on the terrace. Mary bit her tongue. Bill had meeting at school tonight. Quiet evening."

The evening of November twenty-first was a quiet

evening. She wrote to her father and explained that going to Maryland for Thanksgiving was impossible because I was in bed with mumps and had a temperature of a hundred and three. She wrote to Mrs. Whitney about the plays they should see in New York. We listened to Guy Lombardo on the radio. I wonder if she thought of my promise to take her to the Roosevelt Grill. We talked about *Too Late the Phalarope* and she read aloud several beautiful passages. She arranged the things I would need for the night and went upstairs. I could hear the doors open and close as she went from room to room, tucking in the covers to keep snug three innocent worlds of dreams.

Then she sat on the edge of her bed and wrote her five lines for the day. What does a person write if the lines are her last? Is there the last, or do we confuse changes with ultimates? This had been another uneventful day: "Kip and D.B. went to the Greiners' for the day. Mary went to Molly's this afternoon and to dinner. Loomises and Porzelts here this afternoon. Evening of relaxing. Funny attack in throat."

It was almost November twenty-second when she came quietly down the stairs. She mentioned a strange choking sensation in her throat. I told her to call the doctor, but she hesitated. She said she hated to bother him at such an hour. But I insisted, and she did call. Until he arrived her primary concern was that he give me something to take my temperature down. Soon she could breathe more freely. They enjoyed a pleasant visit. She told the doctor that when I paneled the study I had put one hemlock board in with the pine to make a good game for a party sometime. They looked for the hemlock board.

We had never had a real party. She always talked about it, but I always persuaded her to wait until I had everything finished and just right. This Christmas would be the time. We had not yet had the usual housewarming. The school chaplain had come to bless the house. He read a simple and impressive little service in the Prayer Book which I had never seen. She knew it was there.

I heard the doctor call the school infirmary and tell the nurse to fix a bed for Martha. Martha thought she shouldn't go, but the doctor explained that it would be wise. He didn't want me to get out of bed in case she needed something during the night. The doctor knew. An assistant came and they bundled her up to go. She laughed at the idea that she should be carried. The doctor jokingly assigned his assistant the job of teaching her church-school class when she insisted that she must get in touch with someone early the next morning. They laughed about the new teacher, and soon they were ready to leave. She told me whom to call to get things started in the morning, and where to find the boys' Sunday shirts. I told her she would be back in time, and I said, "Good night."

She said, "I'll see you in the morning." And they were gone.

Our border collie was at the front door when they left, and still his vigil does not end. Through snow, sleet, rain or wind, he remains. He will not go to the back of the house and sleep in his doghouse. He is waiting.

"I'll see you in the morning." What are the last words of one who has spoken only of kindness and love? What are the last words of one who has loved God and all His children? "I'll see you in the morning."

The flood rises almost without notice. There is a whirling, gentle and silent. The right side of the heart pumps blood into the lungs; the left side of the heart pumps the blood out of the lungs. If something happens to the left side of the heart there is "a funny attack in the throat." The spirited warm blood rises higher and higher. There is a whirling, gentle and silent. She has gone to sleep; she breathes faster but does not move or waken; she breathes no more. The flood has risen slowly; it is gentle and silent. The spirited warm blood cools. A faint gurgling swallow, and a slow whirling downward—into the lap of God.

It hasn't been an hour yet since they left. A car comes up the hill. They have forgotten something. The front door opens and the rector comes through the back hall.

"Bill, I have some bad news for you."

I start to turn on the light, but he stops me.

"Martha is gone. I know it sounds so terribly trite, but she went as peacefully and quietly as one can go. She went while she slept. The doctor is here and wants to come in."

In the semidarkness, silhouetted by the dim light that came from the end of the hall, stood a man of God. Here stood a man whose life was consecrated to bringing good news to the world. The flood tide whirled in silence. I was passing "through the waters." And in this darkness the man of God would have taken my place in the torrent. Above the gurgling swallow of the slipping of my world into these thickened waters, his voice rose, calmly and strong, as he prayed, "And let Thy light eternal shine forever upon her." In the darkness, he could see a light above the levee, a Watchman with a lantern in his hand, a star in the fingers of God. "And through the rivers, they shall not overflow thee."

"The doctor wants to come in."

He went out, and the doctor came and sat on the edge of the bed. He didn't say anything. That was right. His breathing rose above the heavy silent movement of the maelstrom. A message comes from the sound of breathing in the dark. They would have stayed through the night, but, somehow, they knew it was right for them to go. When a man prays, he prays alone; and when he curses God, he curses God alone.

Some things are too long even when one would never have them end. Hammered from the dream of what cannot be into the reality of what is on the crest of mad waters, the night is forever. How can the dawn delay so long? "In the morning" does not come by the clock. The gray visitor will leave his sister Grief to diffuse the dawn, but a shadowed remnant of this night will prevent another day for me. The tomorrows for which we build are gone.

Suddenly I am an old man. I will not plan again. What did I do to make this price necessary to balance the books with God? Why is one sick and the other dies? Martha made the world better. Doesn't God want the world better? There is a confusion of thought, a struggle to rise above the crest, a will to sink. The deep, heavy emptiness of these soundless hours is stirred. Faint footsteps, a door opens, the footsteps pass the bathroom door. Kip is going to his mother's room. The long night is ending. Yet I would have it longer. Now Kip, David, and Mary will be pulled into the turbulent waters.

If this were a morning, such as the mornings we have known, Kip would follow a routine which has been part of our joy. He'd go from room to room to see that everyone is where he should be. If he finds a book open, turned face down on the night table, he will mark the page properly with the flap of the dust cover, put the book exactly at the corner of the table and go on to the next room. In Mary's room he would pick up her blue blanket from the floor and put it back on her pillow, and perhaps line up the shoes. In David's room he would rearrange the plastic Indians— white horses and black Indians on one side, blue horses and brown Indians on the other. He would have other things to put in order in David's room, for when David goes to bed, he takes two guns and rides either with the Lone Ranger or away from the bad men. Long ago we learned not to throw bathrobes over the ends of the beds, for this was an offense to end sleep. Last summer we slept in the summerhouse once without telling him, but he came and found us. Now he will come down and ask for Mommy.

This is a different morning. He will not announce proudly at breakfast, "I have straightened up the house."

I cannot tell them separately. They must all come down together. Each day Kip saves a little love, a little energy, a few "thanks yous" to begin the next day. Today Kip will save the broken pieces of his heart. David is a year and a half younger than Kip. He will be seven in six more weeks; he rides harder and sleeps longer. David puts all his love, all his energy, all his "thank yous" into each day. Today his heart will break and there will be no pieces big enough to save. I must remember to tell whoever comes in where to find the Sunday shirts.

Mary, whom the boys fondly call Sis, will be the last to awaken. She went with Mommy yesterday to get the invitations for her birthday party. She will be five in seven more days. She will stand between

the boys when they come into the room. She will be
confused and hurt. She will tell me many times in
the days to come that Mommy is still in the house
because her scarf is on the dresser, or her pen is on
the desk. And after the flood she will be the dove,
bringing the olive branch, showing that the waters
are going down and that the earth remains.

One of the trusty hired women from the school has
come in to get breakfast. The children must not see
her before I have talked to them. She must go quietly
to the kitchen.

Kip is coming down the stairs. I must call him before he goes into the kitchen.

"Kip."

He comes to the door. He has heard someone in the
kitchen.

"What's Mommy doing up so early? Are you
sicker? Why are all the lights on?"

"Kip, go up and get David and Sis. There is something I want to tell you, and I want to tell all three
of you at the same time."

I didn't want to tell them. How could I take out
of their lives something for which there is no sub-
stitute on earth? How could I, within a matter of

seconds, tell them something that would create a wistful yearning to remain in their hearts as long as they live?

They are coming down the stairs, innocently laughing and racing. They are almost at my door.

III

Undertow

The waves reach for the land and would consume it, and underneath the certain pull of the undertow engulfs, confuses, and finally swallows up in the deep dark waters, the thing it has taken in its grasp. The desolation of black depths is boundless and without horizons, measureless without end.

We had always saved pleasant surprises for the morning. If there was a trip or an invitation, it was saved because little minds magnify excitement until sleep is pushed as far away as possible. So I knew why there was laughter on the steps. They knew Mommy was up early to take them to visit their cousins. They would go away for the day so Daddy could rest.

They pushed through the door. Mary was the last to get in, but instinctively she took her place between the boys. I noticed that the white collars of their little plaid bathrobes were dirty. In a second there was a long silence that reached to the ends of the earth and back again.

"We're going to Pittsfield to see Uncle Andy and Aunt Margaret."

Mary spoke. She was youngest. Anticipated joy is measured by the gauge of innocence. There is a difference between five and seven. David and Kip were questioning only with their eyes.

"No, Uncle Andy and Aunt Margaret are coming down here this morning. Mommy is not in the kitchen. A friend has come to get breakfast for us. Last night Mommy got sick and the doctor took her to the infirmary so she would have the nurse to take care of her during the night. She went to sleep at the infirmary and she died in her sleep. She has gone to Heaven and we won't see her again for a long time. We will live the way she did. Someday we will see her again in Heaven."

Kip's heart broke slowly, and it bled. He looked behind him and wiped away his tears. At the same time he spoke for all, "We want Mommy." David's heart broke so quickly there was no time for bleeding. There was not a single tear. Only the quick draining of the color from his face showed me the thousand shattered pieces of the little urn that had held so much love. Mary knew, but I could not tell her feeling for she was young and her heart was still grafted on to God. In days to come, I would see the taproot of her heart find firm foundations in simplicity (which yesterday I would have called frailty). In the question, "But when is Mommy coming back?" I saw the earth slip from beneath her. She too was swept into the flood.

Strange, I had thought they would ask more questions. The torrent swept them out and away from me. They did not believe. They looked first in the kitchen. Then I heard the doors open and close as they were swept from room to room, searching for some familiar sign on the landscape of their lives which had become so suddenly strange and unknown to them. Kip struggled in confidence. He had seen things as they should be so many mornings before. David moved numbly, because he knew nothing else to do. Mary followed the boys.

They have visited all the rooms. Now they are back. I must guard them against change. A change of routine creates insecurity. Insecurity could never be erased.

"Mommy is not here." David spoke, but there was doubt in the way he spoke.

"Mommy's spirit is here, and it will be here as long as we are. It will never leave us." I knew he did not understand. "Now you must go to breakfast, and then get ready for Sunday School."

"But Mommy isn't here to take us."

"The Smiths will take you."

By now people were in the house. I knew they were answering questions, and I hoped they could find better answers. They were glorious people, they would have given back the love and kindness which Martha had given them. They would have patched the levee, turned this tide. They proved their magnificence in little things. The gaudy, insignificant details of earth they managed. They came quietly to the door and knocked. "Please let us know if we can help." And then they go away for there was nothing else to do. One by one they showed how the heart of a village is broken. Each had known her smile, her selflessness, her kindness, her love.

The children have gone to church. Somebody will teach Martha's class. My children will again hear that God loves us. Can they believe that God loves us today? Will other children hurt them with cruel, meaningless questions?

Can I believe that God knows and loves? In the undertow God has destroyed what He had given me. Before my very eyes He has destroyed my world. I am conscious of the cruelness of it. If this tide must come, why am I not able to stand up? Could I not have gone to the infirmary with her? Could I not have been strong before the children? Why did He bind me, make me helpless, at this hour? This is the one day, of all days, I would have chosen to stand upon my feet. I have been wronged by God. In my bitter blackness there is no light.

Time has become a web. In that web another gray November day crawled slowly over Cobble Hill, Segar Mountain, Mt. Algo, and has gone. I think of Martha. How happy she seemed when she left. Her last thought was of those she loved and not of herself. How casually I had said good night. How sure she was of the morning. God kept me from standing by her side, from taking her at the last in my arms, from telling her how much I love her. Yet was this important? When you love someone, do you always have to tell them? Don't they really know?

Out there across the twilight she knew I loved her.

She had always known. As I brooded upon the hills as they disappeared in darkness, I wondered why the God above these hills had added to the flood an undertow and with it was destroying the only foundation I had stood upon.

The footsteps through the house were muffled.

The people's voices came only faintly in to me. The children were in bed. I felt that somehow they would sleep. Would they dream? Could I in some way heal their wounds? God would heal their pain? Kip was probably biting his lip, and wondering. David would cry to himself, and repeat his prayers over and over. Mary, confused, would lie in her little bed. She'd think, perhaps, that she was dreaming before her eyes were closed. She would not understand. Here in darkness I would have helped those who, for many tomorrows, would bring the light to me.

The great waves, the emptiness of silence and of time, made up the night. If my temperature went down, the doctor would let me go to the funeral. On the drab brown house across the street from the church the porch lights are burning now. Tomorrow night the villagers will walk in, stand silently and ponder life's puzzles, and then return to their homes. I will not be with them. Martha will understand. Now she understands so much more.

Martha and I had often talked about teaching and education. We had come to feel that the purposes of the education of man were determined even before the "foundations of the earth were laid." Education meant only one thing—Christian education.

The philosophy of education began with Socrates. Education should guide men in those pursuits which make the soul as good as possible. But Socrates lived in a pagan world. A historical event on a hill called Golgotha, outside the City of Jerusalem, added a third dimension to education. The good was not enough.

How many times I had told my students that "the good is not enough." During fifteen years of teaching I have said that there were good men and good citizens, doing what they thought best for their state and their fellow men, on that hill outside Jerusalem. But down from the Cross has come a new meaning for education, an interpretation of the purposes for man. For there the world had been overcome. True, we live in a two-story world. We render "unto Caesar the things which are Caesar's; and unto God the things that are God's," but our education must take us above the first story. The value of our education will be weighed for each of us at some unknown hour beyond our "threescore and ten" when we will need that most important of all educational skills, the skill of finding what we want. All these things I had told my students.

Once I gave a class a horrifying assignment to rouse and move them. I required each of them to write his obituary as he supposed it would appear the day after that unknown time. This world is not important, I had told them.

Martha had been the soul of my teaching. Once, after she came to the door of my classroom for something, she had told me that the smile I wore in the classroom was the brightest she had ever seen me wear. She knew I loved my work. We had not envied the world's goods, often more plentiful for others than for teachers.

Waves of doubt now beat upon me. What will I do? Those things I taught no longer support me. By now my students have been told that Martha is dead. It was announced today in chapel. Will they remember my words? Will they expect me to show the readiness I had taught them to achieve. I must want more than God has taken away this day. There must be more. But in the dark flood there is no light.

In the night I ask for water, for the waters around me are bitter. Someone brings it to me. I know the doctor will not let me get up. I want to stand up. A story comes back to me of how the Brontë sisters tried to make their brother, Branwell, stand up to die— one last attempt to find in him a will, a strength, which in his fruitless, wasted life he had not shown. It was a strange story to mingle with a memory of Martha. All her glory was before me, but I could not separate the light and the dark. Morning was coming on, and out of my window I could see the mountains again, and now I knew that God had seen them through the night.

IV

Ebbtide

The man of God, the rector, came in the morning and brought Martha's engagement ring. Her hand and the hand of God were above us. There came to the waters a silence. The tide would pull away in that silence, and time would heal the torn earth where we stood.

This I did not yet know, but man learns in loneliness, in time, in silence. Sorrow makes a day long, and this was a long, empty day. Kip and David went to school as usual, and Mary went to nursery school. I sensed delay and confusion in their starting out. Before they went down the hill, Martha had always heard their morning prayers. This morning jackets, caps, gloves and books were enough to occupy the kind people in the house.

Kip had a favorite prayer. It was only when he wanted to save time to look for a lizard at the pond, halfway down the hill, that he said another. I went over his prayer for him after he was gone:

> A whole new day is mine to live in,
> To work and play, to get and give in,
> A chance to learn, a chance to grow,
> And much depends on me, I know.
>
> I thank thee, God, for power to choose
> The right from wrong, for chance to use
> My day, and all the strength it brings,
> In doing happy, worthwhile things.
>
> So when the hours of day have flown,
> I pray I may have stronger grown;
> That I can say when night brings rest,
> "Dear God, I tried to do my best."*

David, who has always seemed to sense a fear of the world and of being hurt, has his favorite prayer too:

I think God's love is great enough the whole wide world
    to hold,
The great and wise, the young and small, the helpless
    and the old.
All little creatures out of doors, place in God's love can
    find.

*Then keep me ever in that love that I may grow more
    kind.*
O let me never find my fun in any play that gives,
*Through act of mine, terror or pain to anything that
    lives.**

Mary always prays as though she thinks God has
to catch the bus. She hurries to get through, as though
He might miss the last line:

> *I believe in God above,*
> *I believe in Jesus' love,*
> *I believe His Spirit too,*
> *Comes to tell me what to do;*
> *I believe that I should be*
> *Kind and gentle, Lord, like Thee.**

I had only heard their morning prayers on the two
mornings each year when Mommy was in New York.
Then they would also ask God to "help Mommy have
a good time, come safely home, and bring us something nice."

On Monday the doctor said I could not get up to
go to the funeral. The funeral would be on Tuesday
afternoon so as not to interfere with the children's
school routine, and so that Martha's friends from the
school would not have to miss their teaching ap-
pointments. I did not argue with the doctor. I knew

* Permission of Forward Movement Publications.

his decisions were made in strength. I knew his respect for a higher Power in all his work.

The children came home from school. Mary brought a scarf into the room and held it up for me to see.

"This is Mommy's scarf. She is still in this house."

Grief is a dark, heavy thing, and hard to penetrate. But David tried. He came in and stood by the bed for a long time. What he said had to be free from "terror or pain to anything that lives." He needed time.

"Mommy will ask God to make you well, and that's what we want. When are you going to shave?"

Christopher, who preferred to be called Kip, was busy getting ready for a Thanksgiving play at school. He needed a quill such as the Pilgrims had used. He cornered a goose in the fence below the pond, and then came in to show me the large wing feather that would write after the end was sharpened. He said that he had asked his friends at school not to talk about Mommy being dead.

Once he had gone with me to the freeze-locker plant. We had seen a lamb that had been slaughtered. On the way home he said we would never mention it again.

Through my window I could see a dead birch tree that had fallen on the fence. I would move it when I got up.

Another gray November day folded, condensed, and was distilled into night. The devout and the curious would be walking through the door. They would be going in and coming out from seven to nine. They would be seeing for the last time, but I would go on seeing forever. I would see life, love, and light. My feud with God was passing with the long tide.

The people in the house moved quietly. After the children went to bed there was stillness, a heavy vapor of nothingness, pressing down upon loneliness. I had asked one of the people to bring me the Prayer Book from the bedside table upstairs. I would remember later to tell my students that there comes a time when the thing we ask for is often something that we had considered a little thing.

Tuesday the children went to school. The people moved slowly about the house. Then the children came home. The boys put on their Sunday shirts. Strange hands braided Mary's hair. Soon it was time for them to leave. Two of the kind people stayed behind to keep the house. Somewhere out there in the house they sat quietly.

Now Martha's friends and my friends gather silently. Three pale little faces turn toward the aisle. The minister, so calm that night—three days ago, now ages—is following the slow march. His voice is clear and deep, coeval with the sound of creation's dawn:

I am the resurrection and the life, saith the Lord: he that believeth in Me, though he were dead, yet shall he live: and whosoever liveth and believeth in Me, shall never die. . . .

I know that my Redeemer liveth . . . yet shall I see God . . . and not as a stranger.

The Lord gave, and the Lord hath taken away; blessed be the Name of the Lord. . . .

Christopher will face the front again. He wishes no one could see him raise his hand to his cheek. David looks at the floor. He still faces the aisle, but he cannot change. He is fixed and motionless. Mary sees her nursery school teacher across the aisle and manages a faint smile.

The certain voice, born out of conviction and consecration, continues:

For a thousand years in Thy sight are but as yesterday when it is past, and as a watch in the night. . . .

So teach us to number our days, that we may apply our hearts unto wisdom. . . .

Martha had used only two parts of her threescore and ten; her birthday was just last Thursday. Christopher had crashed into the tea wagon and demolished some of her teacups, so for her birthday we had bought some new ones. Now they will gather dust in the cupboard. One day I will give them to Mary.

The voice of the man who would have borne our grief drowns out David's faint choking sob:

God is our hope and strength, a very present help in trouble.
Therefore we will not fear, though the earth be moved, and thought the hills be carried into the midst of the sea;
Though the waters thereof rage and swell, and though the mountains shake at the tempest of the same.
There is a river, the streams whereof make glad the city of God.

A dozen years ago we had stood before another altar and said, "For better, for worse, for richer, for poorer, in sickness and in health, to love and to cherish, till death us do part. . . ." All that was good she had brought. All that was good she has left for us. Death cannot part us.

On the morning Christopher was born, I had listened to a brown thrasher, singing to the dawn. The thrasher had flown away even while I waited, but the song remained. I would have it forever. Death could not part us.

Almost every Sunday evening, after the laundry list was made out, Martha used to play the piano. She had many favorite hymns. Now her friends are singing one of them:

> *The King of love my shepherd is,*
> *Whose goodness faileth never;*
> *I nothing lack if I am His,*
> *And He is mine for ever.*

> *Where streams of living water flow,*
> *My ransomed soul He leadeth,*
> *And where the verdant pastures grow,*
> *With food celestial feedeth.*

> *Perverse and foolish oft I strayed,*
> *But yet in love He sought me,*
> *And on His shoulder gently laid,*
> *And home, rejoicing, brought me.*

> *In death's dark vale I fear no ill*
> *With Thee, dear Lord, beside me;*
> *Thy rod and staff my comfort still,*
> *Thy cross before to guide me.*

Thou spread'st a table in my sight;
Thy unction grace bestoweth:
And O what transport of delight
From Thy pure chalice floweth!

And so through all the length of days
Thy goodness faileth never:
Good Shepherd, may I sing Thy praise
Within Thy house for ever.

Sometimes I used to fold my hand over hers when we prayed, and my prayer was better for it. The last prayer is being said now.

The children have come home. They did not see the coffin carried out; they saw it last just about arm's reach from where Christopher, David, and Mary stand in their junior choir stalls. I often wonder if they think of it.

On the day after Thanksgiving Martha was folded into the hill that looks down on Rock Creek, in Rockville, Maryland, "in sure and certain hope of the Resurrection unto eternal life." And she is with us, healing the scars that were left after we had passed "through the waters."

V

Mist

Sometimes the valley that lies below us fills up quickly with a foamy white mist that hovers near the earth so that, while we can see the hill down to the sheep barn and the mountains around us, the river and trees and houses are buried in the thick white. Sometimes the white mist pours over the mountains and hides their tops from us, and then hangs there above us. But the white void never seems to hide the depths and the heights at the same time. So in the days to come the mist of doubt and fear and hurt would fill in the world in which we groped, and the mist of understanding would hang down upon the mountains; but when one came, the other cleared.

On the fourteenth day after I had gone to bed, the

doctor let me get up. I wanted to walk through the house alone. I wanted to be there only with the children. So the last kind helpful neighbor left and we were alone. There was a strange fascination that sent me from room to room, looking for something, some strength, some power that would be there, something that would fill up emptiness. Why didn't Mary come yelling that the boys were teasing her? Why didn't the boys start a fight in the basement? Usually about every half-hour we could expect a good argument or free-for-all over some toy. Now there was only the dull hum and rattle of the toy train as it went round and round in what seemed an endless monotony. Wouldn't David ever arrange the plastic Indians to hold up the train? Why didn't I hear the shouts of the cowboys as they galloped in to scatter the Indians? Why doesn't Mary talk to her dolls as she plays?

Finally, I could stand the still emptiness and dark silence no longer. I walked to the edge of the sheep pasture and looked down into the lower meadow. It was a blotter-type December day. The earth was wet and the white mist hung over the tops of the mountains. Down in the lower pasture a young ewe was being bred by Heathcliff, our ram. The ewe was a spring lamb, only eight months old. She had gotten into the wrong field; I didn't want the ewe lambs bred. To breed them too young affects their growth, and they remain too small to be satisfactory and productive as mothers. But she would have a late lamb, and it would be a tiny little thing. Here was life beginning, and the pattern of creation was going on. The sound of the bells came faintly up the hill. The heavy dampness of the earth and air seemed to soak up the very sound of them.

Standing on the hill, below the mist, I wanted to drive through my mind a total picture of all the happiness of the twelve years we had had together. There was no total picture. There were little fragments, minutes that now separated themselves from time and space, and became what they had been—love.

The memory of the brown thrasher, singing in the early dawn, outside a hospital window, came back to me again. Why did I remember this so clearly, when I couldn't even remember the words of the doctor when he had told me that we had a son? I think I remember it because the imperishable song of the brown thrasher was the same as the silent, inexpressible song that leaped into my heart from Martha's thankful and worshipful eyes when I first saw her after Kip was born.

I remembered how I sat in the back of the chapel and silently wept when she had played the part of Mary in a nativity play. People had written her letters about how beautifully she had played the part; the boys at school had given her a lovely, living flower that she had kept blooming so long. I had given her a single rose, as I had done many times before and later. Now I pondered why I had given her only one rose. When I had known her only a month, I had sent her the first rose. It was the opening night of a little theater production in Staunton, Virginia. It is so strange that these little things crowd out the problems that I must go back to the house and face. In another hour I must start the potatoes for dinner, my first meal for the children.

One bright October day comes back to me. I called Martha from school and asked her if she would like to ride to Sharon. It's only a twenty-minute ride, and I was going to look at some ewes that the Rockridge Farm had for sale. I don't know why I even thought she might like to go, but she was thrilled. We enjoyed autumn at its best, going by the valley and returning by the mountain. Was that morning something aside, something out of the ordinary? It didn't seem so then, but now it comes back and stands alone, apart from all the many rides and trips we had together. I cannot remember what we talked about on the ride. Perhaps she thought I shouldn't buy the sheep and said so. I don't remember. Perhaps I remember it because it was one of those rare times in life when for a fleeting moment togetherness is intensified by an unexplainable power that utilizes the singleness of love and the immense completeness of God's design in the beauty of autumn. And here, leaning against the gate, surrounded by a void that stretches dark and heavy upon time, a few minutes of seeming insignificance rise up in brightness. Later I would understand how time and loneliness flash back, because we could not endure a glorious panorama of all our life together.

Back in the house, I moved on leaden feet from chore to chore. What would the first meal be like? What would I do wrong? Baked potatoes and lamb chops, green beans out of our freezer that Martha and I had prepared and frozen. This was our first meal. While I moved between oven door and sink, Mary walked into the kitchen. She stood with her little hands on her hips, looked around, and said, "What can I do to help you?" When I could finally speak without a quiver, I told her that from now on she would have a regular job of setting the table. She went about it with grace and efficiency, and in no time at all she announced that everything was ready. I looked at the table. She had set it for five people.

Mommy's chair was still at its usual place. No one had thought to move it, and perhaps there was no reason why it should have been moved. The chair was at that second an awful thing, and yet it was hard for me to put it away from the table and rearrange the four so as to fill the space.

An incident of twenty years before came back to me and made the chair, and the ceremony of moving it—for it was a ceremony—deep and confounding. I had spent part of a summer with a missionary friend, H. E. Wormeldorf, in Pendleton County, West Virginia, which has the distinction of being so far up in the mountains that there is not one foot of railroad in the whole county. Now a scene from the mountains came back to me.

One evening, at graying twilight, we had stopped down the hollow from a log cabin. My friend knew the people and wanted to pay a pastoral call. For in that part of the world if the preacher's car comes along, the people expect the preacher to visit. As we walked up the hollow we could hear the strumming of a banjo and someone singing. The song was about a vacant chair. Before we saw the cabin through the trees we had had a good laugh about the vacant chair. Now I knew that the banjo player had known or would know the depth of his song, that from this time on I would know the universality of sentiment, and that at some moment in our lives we two were coeval with Adam, and that we differ little in our feelings.

All I remember about the meal is that it was almost unbearably endless and quiet. It is a terrible thing when children are quiet, for they are either very sick or very hurt.

During the weeks to come I would painfully watch every mouthful of food and I'd check carefully to see that the milk was drunk. Then in the slow, long weeks Mary would teach me that children eat when they are hungry, and nature does a pretty good job at balancing. I was continually speaking to Mary about her food. "Two pieces of this." "You must eat that." Finally, I decided that I would try silence for one meal. She sat without touching her food. Occasionally she glanced to see if I hadn't forgotten something. After a while she could stand the lack of attention no longer. "Daddy, aren't you going to speak to me about eating?" After that we had no problems with eating habits.

In the long weeks and months conversation came back, and even an occasional dart of sunlight pierced the gray mist of grief. Something I cooked would be as good as Mommy could do it. Something would even look tasty as they learned again to romp their way to the table rather than walk aimless and silent as they had done those first dark days and weeks.

Watching through a long night is seeing a reflective mirror. Things as they were come back and are reflected in the stillness. But the days had to clear. There were so many things to see as they must be. Big things and little things. The children must feel secure in their home, although it stood mocking security, and insecurity was about us and filled up within us.

The little things became important too. When the first laundry came back a lengthy conference was necessary. Whose socks are these? Are the red pajamas yours? Kip and David wore about the same size. Whose is the blue shirt, and whose the white?

Now we must organize. David must have green and blue socks when we buy some more. Kip must have red and yellow socks. David must have blue dress shirts, and Kip must have white. David's flannel shirts must be two plaid combinations; Kip's must be another. Kip must learn to sort the laundry, and all three must learn to put it neatly away in their bureau drawers, each drawer and each portion of a drawer for this or that. We had to partition off the drawers with plywood. The socks belong in this section. We need practice in turning one sock over the other so as to keep pairs in order. Into another section must be put underpants. One side of a drawer is for Sunday shirts and the other side for school shirts. There was so much to do now that everything required organization. While she was washing her teeth, Mary had to learn to think about what dress she would wear the next day. Precious time in the morning did not allow hesitations for decisions.

The things which had always seemed incidental now became so important because Mommy's touch was gone. The boys learned to make their beds, and competed for the weekly reward for neat bed and room. At five Mary could not manage her bed. Yet she did learn very quickly to put her dirty clothes in the hamper and to hang up her dress when she took it off.

The weekly cleaning of the house involved all of us. On Wednesday morning, all books, toys, and other playthings were picked up before schooltime. Late Wednesday afternoon and evening I would clean. On Saturday morning Mary would empty all wastebaskets, and Kip and David would dust the entire house. We learned the value of time, even the value of those odd minutes which we had tossed aside so freely with the much-repeated statement, "I'll do it in a few minutes."

Time slipped by quickly, but waiting for signs of laughter and happiness from the children was long. So many times I saw the truth of Abraham Lincoln's remark: "In this sad world of ours, sorrow comes to all; and, to the young, it comes with bitterest agony, because it takes them unawares. The older have learned to accept it." Too many people falsely believe that a five, a seven, or a nine year old, will forget quickly. Forgetting becomes inactive emptiness, emptiness that fills up from the bottom of the heart like the mist in our valley, or emptiness that pours over the heart like the mist that creeps down over our mountains. But the emptiness can never consume the love that we have with us.

VI

Raindrops

One of the peach trees that we planted in the garden has grown so large that one of the branches hangs out over the pond. I watched the raindrops that had clung long after the rain had stopped. Even after the moon had broken through a gateway in the clouds, they continued to drop into the water. The moonbeams spread upon the tiny ripples and the ever-increasing circles enlarged until they reached the uttermost parts of that narrow world of water.

There in the night I knew that man, a part of the vast creation, could not live in a narrow world. Martha's world had been a wide world of light. "The light shines in the darkness and the darkness has not overcome it."

Now it was nearly Christmas, and even the stars in the broken sky bespoke the joy that so long ago had accompanied the coming of the Light into the world. I waited until I was sure the last raindrop had fallen into the pond. Then I went back to the house to wrap packages, address cards, and think of the hundred and one things I would have to remember during the last four days before Christmas.

Time had seemed so long, yet many things had happened. One of the kind neighbors had had Mary's birthday party for her, and now she was "really five." Kip and David were practicing for the Christmas pageant at the church. I had already seen their Christmas play at school. The schoolboys had gone to their homes for the holidays before I was able to return to my classes. More than half of the three hundred had attended a 6:00 A.M. requiem celebration of the Holy Eucharist for Martha on the morning of her funeral. The student officers of the form I taught had served at the altar. We should have found some way to thank them for all their many kindnesses before they left for vacation, yet, somehow, they must know. On the editorial page of their school paper they wrote:

It takes time to comprehend fully the impact of Martha Armstrong's sudden death. She knew and loved everyone

*on both sides of the bridge [the bridge separates the
school and the village], and everyone on both sides of
the bridge knew and loved her. She was a soul possessed
of boundless love of God and all the people He made.*

They understood. Boys are great because they cannot hide their hearts. They wear their magnificent
souls on their coat sleeves for all to see and read.
Only teachers who are taught so much by them can
fully appreciate them. They, indeed, are the raindrops
which catch a beam of light that broadens and
broadens to brighten the dark recesses of age.

When I went back to stand before my classes in Jan-
uary, I stared out of the window and choked upon every
word. They wrote their pity and their sorrow in their
eyes. Now and then one of them, unable to stand it
any longer, would quietly leave the room. Out of their
weekly allowance of fifty cents for icecream, Coca
Cola, and candy, they gave five hundred dollars to
buy a chapel window. And surely, the following
September, when I stood hovering with Kip, David,
and Mary at the dedication, they knew that we had
learned from them.

Sometimes great problems are solved so simply that
we marvel that there was ever a problem at all. The

first night we were alone after Mommy was gone and after the last kind neighbor had left, I studied Mary's braids carefully after she had gone to sleep. They were neat and tight. I wondered why Martha had bothered to braid anew each morning. Surely, they would hold for a few days until I could learn from someone how to do it. Mary's nursery school teacher would be able to show me. I would ask her tomorrow when I got Mary from school.

When I went up to help Mary dress the next morning I could not believe my eyes. What could have happened during the night? Strings of hair hung down in her eyes. Her braids looked like a rope that had been pulled back and forth over the sharp edge of an angle iron until it was ready to break. I had learned to splice a rope when I was a Boy Scout. Perhaps something of the same principle would work.

After breakfast we started. Something or somebody had woven little webs into this soft and silky hair. Mary stood in silence for a while, and then she began to cry. After the tangles were all out we began to braid, first with two strands. When we finished and secured the ends with rubber bands, it unwound like a spring. The next try was with three strands and it held.

After that we developed a story, and the story re-placed the tears.

Through the bathroom window we could see an old butternut tree with three forks. It had grown over a limestone ledge and there was an opening in the ledge under the tree. No tree is more suitable for the home of elves than an old worm-eaten, deformed butternut that has lived beyond its years and desperately hangs on to life. Dead branches were caught amid living ones, and deserted holes of woodpeckers dotted the half-barkless trunk.

So two elves lived under the old butternut tree. They were good elves because they were weaver elves. They spent their time helping spiders weave webs to catch bad insects. Sometimes, because they loved their work, they would gather tiny dewdrops from leaves and put them on the webs they had made so in the morning we could see the silvery webs along the fence that ran up the hill.

But in winter the elves have no webs to make because all the bad insects, and even the spiders, curl up under the bark of the trees and sleep. And so in order to keep their fingers nimble the little elves come each night while Mary sleeps and weave their little webs which we call tangles. They are not naughty elves. They know that if they do not weave, we would not brush and comb properly, and the tiny dew-drops of oil would not shine in Mary's hair, and it would not be soft and beautiful, but coarse and dull.

The days become weeks and months, and the months become years. There are no more tears at braiding time.

The elves live a varied life. Once one fell from the butternut tree and broke his leg. He was the left-handed elf, so all the webs were on the right side for a while. Sometimes in summer when swimming makes braiding more difficult, the elves, who love Mary's hair so much that they will not stop even though they have to work almost all night to help the spiders, come to work with spider thread still on their hands. This makes terrible tangles when it is interwoven in the hair.

Her braids make her look like Mommy. Someday she will go off to school and cut her hair. But she will still look like Mommy.

Back in the house, in the lonely silence and gloom, away from the stars and the night, I must arrange whatever I can to make Christmas a joyous time for Kip, David, and Mary. In our desperation we must stand together upon a lonely plain back two thousand years in history and gaze upon a star, and be frightened as shepherds were frightened, and finally make our quivering voices heard.

Christmas was the time when Martha heard from all her friends—classmates, her old head mistress from twenty-five years back, people she had kept up with over the years: Dear Martha . . . Your lovely children are just now at the age to make Christmas so much fun for you, I know . . . Dear Martha . . . I think of you often and wish we could arrange a reunion back at Stuart Hall. If you ever get to Ohio . . . Dear Martha . . . It is time again for our annual accounting. This has been a pleasant year for us . . . Dear Martha . . . How you must enjoy your dear children and your lovely home at this season of the year . . . Dear Martha . . . How has the year been with you? They pass so quickly. Your children are beginning to sound so grown-up already . . .

And only the silence answered, "A bruised reed He will not break, and a dimly burning wick He will not quench."

The things which people do at Christmas we did. We mailed out the cards which Mommy had already started to address. We signed them Daddy, Kip,

David, and Mary. We tried to sort the gifts she had already bought for the proper cousins, aunts, and uncles. In the midst of our deciding what to get for this or that friend, David paused and from his little broken heart, "What can we give Mommy for Christmas?"

Be not afraid; for behold, I bring you good news of a great joy which will come to all the people; for to you is born this day in the City of David a Savior, who is Christ the Lord.

So for Mommy's Christmas we built a prayer rail against one wall of the study. We used some pine boards left over when the house was built. We put her picture above the kneeling rail, and over the picture we put a light enclosed by a valance. In the top of the valance we left a small hole, so one thin shaft of light shines upon a small crucifix. (One day we might be thought prospects for the purchase of a splinter from the cross, but that does not disturb us.) When we say our prayers in the morning we kneel there, and at night when we ask God "my soul to keep," we are there.

I know now why Mothers are tired. The energy expended in watching over children is greater than lumbering, hauling stones, and house building combined. I soon learned that if a day was to run smoothly it had to start early. Besides seeing that the collective teeth, which vary from month to month and mouth to mouth, are washed, there is the before-school problem of inspecting faces, fingernails, hands, ears. We felt that a great triumph had been reached when we discovered that the barber's secret for having little boys leave the barbershop with hair neatly parted and in place was the result of mixing a little waveset with ordinary hair tonic. Now the stream of water from the bathroom to the breakfast table has dried up and the parts are straight with every stubborn sprig in place.

Breakfast has been complicated beyond reason and space by the liberal prize-giving habits of cereal makers. In order to get all the necessary emblems and frogmen needed for a decent collection, there must be at least seven different boxes of the food that makes champions or quick fingers on the trigger. And sometimes all seven boxes have to be on the table at once, for the choice is always from the box most nearly down to the prize.

Some kind manufacturer of vitamin pills will one day make them square, because by the third request "Take your vitamin," one of the three is already the object of a hands and knees' search under the table.

Putting up the Christmas tree had been such a joy for Martha and me. Now it was a race against morning. It was hard to believe she wasn't there. She would almost surely be coming home from the midnight service to help arrange the gifts. She would come downstairs with us in the morning to see the dancing eyes and hear the exclamations of appreciation.

During the nightly walk from room to room, tucking in the covers, a second and a third look, I asked half-audibly, "Why can they not have their mother in the morning?—of all mornings when their hearts should overflow with joy and happiness?" I wondered if they felt the dark silence or whether they dreamed dreams that were children's dreams.

I am the light of the world; he who follows me will not walk in darkness but will have the light of life.

In front of the grocery store a man who was almost a stranger to me had waited just outside the door for me.

"She was always so happy. Whenever I saw her, the car seemed to be full of smiling children. I miss her in the village." And then he was gone because he knew I couldn't say, "Thank you."

The village paper under the headline, "Kent

Mourns Martha Armstrong," had said: "A ...
deep loss pervaded Kent all this week. Unbelievab ...,
Martha Armstrong has left us. . . ."

An editorial with the title, "A Tribute to Martha
Armstrong," was in the form of a letter:

*Dear Martha Armstrong—What a heart-rending trag-
edy to have lost your life out of our lives while you were
still so young and had so much to give, especially the
dear, loving kindness you would have given your little
children and all those who were near to you.*

*How can we help them through this infinitely sad
time of learning to get along without you until they are
old enough to carry on your gentle spirit for you—that,
in time will help them.*

*For now, perhaps, the love we have in our hearts for
you may help a little. We would give it in full measure.*

How long is a week? I worried about the time the
children must spend alone. "The car full of smiling
children." Now they would have to come home from
school on the bus and wait one hour, two hours—
how many hours for a child?—until I came. What
would they do? How many times a day had the question been asked, "What can I do now?"

We organized the little jobs that could be done
after school. We wrote the doctor's telephone number
in big numbers so he could be called if someone were

hurt. We learned how to dial the fire department quickly. Responsibility became a part of little minds.

Now I know that it is good for children to be alone. They learn to entertain themselves. The world is full of people who are afraid of leisure. They hide from themselves. They fear their own company. Perhaps Kip and David, wandering at the edge of the woods, playing alone in the basement or in the sheep barn, and Mary, talking to her dolls or playing school, will not be afraid of silence when they meet it at some far distant tomorrow.

Christmas morning came after the long night. Kip awakened David and Mary and they came down together, for one must not see before the other. Joy danced in their eyes and trembled like a flickering candle, but did not go out. "And this will be a sign for you. . . ."

It had turned very cold in the night, and when the sun came up over Segar Mountain all the raindrops were turned to silver and all the trees were Christmas trees. The world was still, except for the tinkle of the sheep bells down in the pasture. Beyond the world there was a Shepherd, and there "beside the still waters" Martha saw the dancing joy that "trembled like a flickering candle, but did not go out."

VII

Covenant

There is a sense of expectancy in children that mystifies us because we do not know the depth of their faith. Kip, David, and Mary expected Mommy to come back. Kip searched in silence. Many a morning I would hear his footsteps as he went to the room where he had always found her. David spoke openly and looked, not secretly, and without a hint that it might be in vain. He would come up the hill from school, open the door and call, "Mommy." Then he would go through the downstairs rooms, go up to Mommy's room, and slowly, without a word, come down and go to the kitchen for his milk and cookies. Mary was confident. "When is Mommy coming back?" was asked many times each day for many

75

days. Her expression of confidence increased rather than decreased.

There was a contagion in their sense of expectancy. In the long nights I would think, It is Thursday and she will be coming home from her bridge group . . . it is Tuesday night, and she will be coming home from her reading club . . . it is Sunday afternoon, and she will soon be down from her nap and take the children for a walk. There was silence and a deep quiet, but there was no familiar footstep.

How could I answer Mary's question so she would understand? How could I convince David so that he would open the door and say "Daddy" rather than "Mommy"? How could I persuade Kip, without speaking openly, that it was useless for him to get up at five o'clock in the morning and look for "Mommy" in her room? Finally I tried to put a great chapter from history into words that they could understand:

When Christ was on earth the people who became his dear friends expected Him to become a leader or even a King. All their lives they had heard the story of how one day a Messiah, a Saviour, would come. They remembered some of the very words, "And He shall be as the shadow of a great rock in a weary land." To us the shadow of a great rock doesn't mean much because we have lots of trees and we have houses. But in the world into which Christ was born many people lived out of doors a great deal of the time. They drove caravans over the trade routes that crossed barren country and deserts, or moved their flocks of sheep from one rugged slope to another where there were no trees and very little grass. So to these people the shadow of a great rock meant getting out of the cold wind at night or escaping for a few moments the scorching sun during the day.

Peter, James, John, and all the other people who became friends of Christ had heard this and many more wonderful things about the Saviour who would come. They had also heard their parents read the words of the prophet how He, too, would die: "like a lamb that is led to the slaughter." Kip, you know how terrible it was to see the lamb slaughtered that time when we went to the freeze locker?

"And they made His grave with the wicked."

You see how strange it is? They had heard that He would help them. He would bring peace to their land and they wouldn't have to be afraid of cruel rulers and wicked soldiers any more. But they had also heard that He would die. But, somehow, they just couldn't believe that part of the story.

Well, one night Christ was arrested. The people who arrested Him said He was a trouble-maker, and was teaching people that they didn't have to obey the law. When He was arrested all His friends ran. They were afraid of the soldiers. One of His friends was named Mark, and he just barely got away. One of the soldiers grabbed his robe, but Mark ran out of his robe and ran home in his underwear to hide. And one of His friends, Peter, loved Christ so much that he just couldn't run and hide. He slipped through the gate to the governor's palace to see what was going to happen to Christ. While Peter stood in a crowd of people around the fire in the courtyard, somebody recognized him and said he was one of the trouble-makers. Peter was so scared that he lied. He said he did not know Christ. Then Peter slipped away and hid like all the rest.

Now don't stop to ask questions, or we will never get the story finished.

The next morning all the dreams of peace and justice that the friends of Christ had expected Him to bring were ended. He was put to death. When the soldiers who had put Him to death had marched back down to Caesarea, where their barracks were, the friends of Christ came out of hiding to see where He was buried. Peter was one of the friends who went to the tomb. In those days graves weren't dug down into the ground, but back into a hill, and a big stone was used to close up the tomb. When His friends got to the tomb, they found that it was empty.

Now they were even more afraid. They didn't know what to think.

On the days which followed, Christ's friends would talk of Him. They remembered what He had said to them and the kind, little things He had done for them. But, most of all, they remembered how much they loved Him and how much more He loved them.

You remember Mark, who escaped from the soldiers in his underwear? Mark said to the others, "I don't think Christ has left us. I feel that He is with us and that He will never truly leave. Everything He said I remember. His Spirit is in this room. His Spirit is with me always."

The others felt the same way. Christ would always be near them. And one day in Heaven they would see Him again.

Now that's the way it is with Mommy. She won't come back to this house. She won't come back here to this world. We don't have to look for her any more. We are just like Christ's friends. Mommy's love is still with us and one day we will see her again.

Children are not bridled and curbed by time. What was yesterday is still the present to them. In their sense of expectancy tomorrow is also now. Hours, days, months, and years are not real in a child's mind. Their minds are filled with the wonder of a trip, an important event like a toy, or even a sorrow. But these things are not catalogued according to yesterday or today or tomorrow. Mommy was dead. It was not yesterday. It was not past. How could they be taught that their now is of so little consequence and "a thousand years are but as yesterday when it is past and as a watch in the night?"

The afternoon after the story Kip came in from skating. "Daddy, was Christ before or after Washington's men at Valley Forge?"

"Christ lived two thousand years ago, and Washington's men were at Valley Forge only about one hundred and seventy years ago."

"Then that's why they lived, no shoes or warm clothes. I'm frozen. If Christ hadn't helped them they couldn't have stood it."

Children reveal to us our closeness to Adam; they reveal the universal heritage of all mankind. Their joys and their sorrows, their hopes and disappointments, bring brightly before us—and not "through a glass darkly"—the struggle of men's souls to find and be close to God.

Between the sewing on of buttons, the swearing at manufacturers for making zippers that stick, the packing of Mommy's clothes to send to earthquake victims in Greece, and the burden of overwhelming problems that we thought could never be solved, it seemed that the long winter was filled with questions. Sometimes they were asked when I made the round at night after the teeth were washed and the prayers were said. Sometimes they came suddenly in the middle of a game. Sometimes they were born out of something that was said at school. They were the questions that Adam asked, the questions that man has encompassed or by-passed with myths since man first walked the earth. They were the questions that hovered over the hill country of Judea after the mist had lifted above the Mount of Olives and the Master was gone.

"Where did Mommy go when she died?"

We don't know where Mommy went; all we know is that she is somewhere with God. But there is a story that gives us some idea of where she went.

When Christ was put to death, two other men were put to death at the same time, one on either side of Christ on the crosses. When they had been hanging on the crosses a long time, and could not endure the pain much longer, one of the men turned to Christ and swore at Him, saying, "Are you not the Christ? Save yourself and us!" The person on the other cross was ashamed of the way Christ had been spoken to. He rebuked the criminal who had cursed Christ and said, "Do you not fear God, since you are under the same sentence of death? . . . and we indeed justly. . . . but this man has done nothing wrong." Then he turned to Christ and said, "Jesus, remember me when you come in your kingly power." And Christ turned to him and said, "Truly, I say to you, today you will be with Me in Paradise." The word paradise means garden, a garden of peace and rest. When St. Paul was writing to some Christians who were trying very hard to get a church organized in the city of Rome, where being a Christian meant being torn to pieces by wild animals in the arena if the soldiers found out about it, he said, "But if we have died with Christ, we believe that we shall also live with him. For we know that Christ being raised from the dead will never die again; death no longer has dominion over Him."

So wherever this place of peace and rest is, Mommy is there, and she is free of all the temptations and sin that we have on earth, and she goes "from strength to strength in the life of perfect service," which is, I believe, loving and glorifying God.

I know this is too hard for you to understand, but you really don't have to understand. You can't, and you won't even when you get big. But if you know it, that is enough.

Some stories mean more than they can ever say. Some questions are answered by silence only.

What does a child know about sin? How could I answer David's persistent question, "Why did Mommy die?" Death, judgment, hell, and Heaven—how gloriously has wisdom been confined that we might not know.

David, we all must die, and if we are Christians we must look upon death as a "sleep with our fathers." That means the people who have died before us. We must all die because our life on this earth is only a period of getting ready to be with God. When God made the world He knew that it was incomplete without love. So He created man—us—that He might love us and we love Him. Now He couldn't make us just to love Him. He had to make us free so that we could love Him of our own free will. If we had not been made free, our love to God would be nothing. We would be like slaves and puppets. When God made man—us—free, man turned away from God and began to love things of the earth and his own ways better than God and God's ways. That is sin. Death is what we have to pay for this sin. But God loves us so much that He did not want us to be dead. So He sent Christ to die for us so that we can rise up at the resurrection and live.

You will understand this better when you are older and study all the things that man has studied. As we study we move toward the truth, but the truth is God. We do not find it all in this world, except the part that God has given us to know through the Prophets' dreams and Christ's revelations. We really know, but it is not put in books. It is put in our hearts.

In your heart you know that Mommy died because God is love, and He is right, and He is just, and He is merciful, and we are all His children. A father does what he does for his children because he loves them.

What can a child know of death, of hell, of judgment, of Heaven? For a child judges not, and where a child is—is Heaven not there?

There is an end to winter. The crows gather stubble in the field and carry it to the mountain for a nest. The chickadee begins its long-trilled whistle. The sheep begin to search the damp spots that thaw early for sprigs of new grass. The children bring their friends home from school to see the new lambs, and the children and the lambs play on the hill together. The crust of the earth breaks and the flowers bloom. Dark clouds roll and crash upon the mountains, and it is April. After the rain a rainbow frames the highest part of the sky. It has no beginning and it has no end.

Martha loved spring so much. The flowers now bloom untouched and die upon the stem. There is no one to bring them to the house. But Kip and David and Mary know that she sees and enjoys them, for she is in a garden where flowers neither wilt nor die upon the stem, and their brightness does not fade.

Therefore will we not fear, though the earth be moved, and though the hills be carried into the midst of the sea; though the waters thereof rage and swell, and though the mountains shake at the tempest of the same.

I'll keep the children quiet so you can rest . . . This will be a typical later November day . . . Footsteps from room to room, tucking in the covers to keep snug three innocent worlds of dreams . . . What does a person write if it is the last? Is there the last, or do we confuse changes with ultimates? . . . This has been another uneventful day . . . I'll see you in the morning . . . The flood rises almost without notice . . . There is a whirling, gentle and silent . . . a faint gurgling swallow . . . a slow whirling downward . . . into the lap of God.

A love, a brown thrasher's song, a child's heart breaking, a shadow that light on earth does not dispel, a question that silence answers, the heaviness of time, a window, a door open . . . a light above the levee, the Watchman with a lantern in his hand . . . and let thy light eternal shine forever upon her . . .

Fear not for I have redeemed thee. I have called thee by thy name, thou art mine. When thou passest through the waters, I will be with thee; and through the rivers, they shall not overflow thee. . . .

The folds of night are shaken by the tinkling of the sheep bells in the lower pasture, the last tiny lamb is born and sleeps beside its mother. Beyond the bounds of space and time, but within the bounds of children's certain dreams, the Shepherd stands watch "beside the still waters."